DREAM INTERNSHIPS!

IT'S NOT _WHO_ YOU KNOW...
IT'S _WHAT_ YOU KNOW!

Secrets of how to get _your foot_ in the door

DREAM INTERNSHIPS! It's Not *Who* You Know... It's *What* You Know!
Secrets of How to Get Your Foot in the Door

For book orders, author appearance inquiries and
interviews, contact us by mail at:

Thurgood Marshall College Fund
Re: Dream Internships!
80 Maiden Lane
Suite 2204
New York, NY 10038
Tel: (212) 573-8888
Fax: (212) 573-8497 or (212) 573-8554

ISBN-13: 978-1-889732-52-7
ISBN-10: 1-889732-52-4

Printed in the United States of America

DREAM INTERNSHIPS!

IT'S NOT _WHO_ YOU KNOW...
IT'S _WHAT_ YOU KNOW!

Secrets of how to get _your foot_ in the door

Dwayne Ashley

Co-author of _I'll Find a Way or Make One:_
A Tribute to Historically Black Colleges and Universities

DEDICATION

For my mother, father and big brothers—
my greatest mentors.

Thank You!

ACKNOWLEDGEMENTS

This book is perhaps one of the greatest contributions to support the transaction of securing an internship or job for any college student. For the past two years, members of my team have helped to shape this important piece of work-Thank You! Born from seven years of experience with more than 1500 students who have graduated from the Fund's Annual Leadership Institute: the lessons we have taught, experienced and perfected come to life. The Thurgood Marshall College Fund's Leadership program served as the research platform for completing this thought provoking work. Thank you to all the students, volunteers and corporate faculty who helped get it right. My sincere thanks to the Thurgood Marshall College Fund's staff individually—you guys are simply great! The Fund would not be what it is today without your support: Beverly, Lisa, Charisma, Shannon, Shineaca, Nicole, Gregg, Joy, Patricia, Atta, Susie, Deborah, Paul, Reggie, Eve, Larry, James, Melissa, Chris, Mykal, Monica, Talesha and Candice-your steadfast commitment and dedication to our students, the "Next Generation of Leaders." Jim Clifton, Chairman and CEO of the Gallup Organization—thank you for consistent advice and counsel. Your leadership, mentorship and sponsorship has continued to fuel new innovation at the Fund. You keep us looking for new opportunities to take our work to the next level of excellence— Thank you and the Gallup team for helping our students soar with the strengths.

Last, members of the Fund's board— Thank you for being more than just directors who come to meetings. Your commitment is evident in your personal connections and involvements with the students and universities.

CONTENTS

1
ARE UNPAID INTERNSHIPS VOLUNTEER SERVICES

Yolonda, junior in college:

I got my first internship after my sophomore year in high school when I was 16 and I have been working in internship positions during the summers and after school for the past five years. I'm a communications major with an emphasis on public relations and I am going into my senior year—yaaaaay me! I'm about to spend this summer in a paid internship with the St. Louis Rams football team.

My internship with the Rams is, I hope, my foot in the door of public relations with professional sports. My intention in this first paid gig in my field is to hone the skills I have acquired in my studies. I don't expect to learn any new technical skills in public relations this summer. I already have a good grasp of how to do PR from my college classes and my other internships, but being with the Rams this summer will give me some very specific knowledge about the difference between the world of college football and the world of professional football. I want to make an impression on the management at the Rams with the quality and professionalism of my work. That will be particularly important because I am female and my career will be in a predominately male environment. I'm also looking to get good letters of recommendation that will help me get the job I want when I graduate next spring. This summer's internship is a major investment of my time with a minimal amount of financial return, but these 10 weeks are an investment in the next ten years of my working life.

Wow! It sounds like Yolanda really has her act together! Notice her feelings about making a lot of money this summer – She doesn't care! Yolanda knows that work and internships are not all about money. Life is not about the Benjamins. I wrote this book because I want all young people to have careers they love, work they enjoy so much that they'd do it even if they didn't get paid. I want their paychecks to be LARGE and to feel like icing on the cake because they are passionate about what they do every day.

How do you find a job you love? One of the very best ways is through internships. Internships are the way "in" to eventually land a career that makes you jump out of bed in the morning, eager to get to work because it doesn't feel like a job.

Do you think Tupac Shakur, Picasso, or Bill Gates earned their fame and fortune by caring only about money? Of course, not! They got rich by doing what they felt they were born to do. The money found them. The purpose of this book is to help every young person find careers that bring them true fulfillment.

Many college students today have seen work in only two ways. Work is a job, a clock-punching drag, necessary to keep food on the table, a roof over their heads and clothes on their backs, without ever providing enough cash to really live large. Or, work is a profession to make money, money, and mo' money.

The chosen few, the actors, rappers, or sports stars get to do what they're born for and make the stupid money. But most of the students I have counseled know better than to bet their lives on making it to the top of the music charts or NBA. Ordinary students can have a career they love with the same passion a pro baller has for making his jump shot or a rapper has for rhyming. The key to finding that career is internships.

What's In It For You?

Internships are a chance to find your dreams before choosing the career that will fulfill you. Internships allow you to explore new worlds of work.

The primary purpose of an internship is to gain, to explore, to see and to make:

- Gain experience
- Explore a possible career path
- See if the environment suits your temperament and see if the specific jobs match your idea of what you thought they would be like
- Make contacts and network with possible employers and others who can help you along the way.

Need a more concrete reason to start brushing up your resume? Employers overwhelmingly tell the Thurgood Marshall College Fund that internships are one of the things they look at first when deciding which new college graduates to hire for full-time positions. Research shows that about 85% of companies that offer internships use them as a recruitment tool. With statistics like that, how could you afford not to intern?

Internships can also be really fun! Kimora, a 20-year-old sophomore recently interned at a power company, "I spent a lot of time in the control room of the power station. It was sooooo cool! I learned a lot about the technology that I'll be using later in my career. Some of it was discussed already in my classes, but hearing and seeing are two different things. It is so much more exciting to experience it all firsthand."

Want another reason to intern? Internships can teach you about who you are, what you want, and what matters to you - but you have to be ready for the challenge.

Two years ago, Josh finished his freshman year at Purdue. He entered, in September, as a clean cut bookworm from the Bronx, New York who wanted to work someday in the business world. He returned home a dreadlocked African American studies major, with a dislike for large corporations. He had new dreams of a career working for a major black cultural institution. His parents were cool. His dad encouraged him to volunteer for the summer in one of the many fine organizations in Harlem, a short subway ride from their home.

In high school, Josh had spent summers and hours after school involved in sports and church activities. He felt he'd made a big mistake by never making that push to have his own money. He felt "soft" among his posse at school because he didn't have a paying gig. That summer after his freshman year, a family friend offered to get him an internship with the prestigious Harlem Book Fair. These internships are coveted because, despite serving long hours, the interns are assigned substantial duties where they get to meet and mingle with the major authors, work with crews for C-Span and other media sponsors, and help manage the crowd of 40,000 book lovers and publishers who attend the event.

Josh was excited about the opportunity. Then a friend got him an interview at Toys R Us. He was the only applicant who showed up in a shirt and tie, and from there he aced the interview and was offered a part-time summer position on the spot. He accepted the position working on the sales floor of their Bronx store and never followed up on the Harlem Book Fair internship. His new college friends thought he was crazy. Why did he make his decision? Because he had started to wonder what he really wanted out of life. How committed was he to his new interests? He had tried so hard to be "cool" that he had gotten away from his true self. Now he suspected that he was simply going through a phase during his first year of college. Josh decided to go with his gut.

He ended up loving his new job and the following summer accepted a sales internship with a major corporation. He had come full circle and was once again interested in the business world. It turned out his desire to be an activist was short-lived. For Josh, taking the Toys R Us job made more sense because he was able to earn some money while getting practical experience in what would ultimately become his profession.

When it comes to what you want to do for a living, there is no "right" or "wrong." Like Josh, you just need to follow your gut and do what you think is going to make you feel happy.

An internship is NOT a Summer Job!

While Yolonda is in St. Louis she will meet coaches, pro ballplayers, journalists and publicists, all of whom can be helpful to her when she finishes school. If her primary concern had been money, she would not have chosen to take the internship. The stipend and room and board will add very little to her savings for college tuition. And it's a PAID internship!

Most internships pay nothing. Entertainment industries - music, film, publishing, radio, TV - tend not to pay and still plenty of ambitious young people are willing to work for nothing just to get their feet in the door. Competition in these fields is stiff. Nonprofit organizations and small companies often don't have the resources to pay much beyond transportation and lunch.

"Not to do" List – How NOT to Think of an Internship

- **Don't think about short-term cash.** Mark Twain said, "Don't let school get in the way of your education." We say, "Don't let a job get in the way of your career." Don't let a dead-end summer job prevent you from getting your foot in the door of the career you dream about.

- **Don't think your fantasy career is out of reach.** It doesn't matter if you are from the projects, the first in your family to go to college, piecing your degree together with evening classes while working at Old Navy or McDonald's. An internship is still a path for you to get that first taste of a career you almost don't even dare to wish for.

- **Don't Give up.** Forget those stories about actors who got their "lucky" break or models who were discovered while shopping at the mall. For the vast majority of us, success will never be about luck. Success requires you to set goals and stay determined.

Reality Check: When you are not a TFB

TFB is a short term for trust fund babies. Don't worry, I'm not going to bore you with Paris Hilton stories. I'm talking about those rare students who live on money their parents and grandparents leave them. Often, internships are a way of life for these young people. They are expected to spend summers working for free in companies and organizations where their family or social connections have made a place for them. It's how the rich and influential make sure that their children grow up to be rich and influential. Later in this book, you'll even read about parents who buy their kids internships!

By the time TFBs are ready to compete for paying jobs, they have the edge on most of their competitors because, while other candidates (like you!) may have degrees from the same schools, the TFBs have the personal relationships with people in the field. They've "networked." They've gotten the hands-on knowledge of daily operations in the profession, and the confidence that comes with familiarity and exposure. They've become "insiders."

We want you to have the same career edge as a TFB. A very real challenge you face is feeling caught between a rock and a hard place: an internship that doesn't pay and the need to earn money for school or to survive while in school. You may feel you must sacrifice the internship that will provide the experience required for the paid position you want after college in order to make it just to next semester.

Conventional wisdom says, "Forget that internship! Right now the bills have to be paid. You need the money; take the bread and butter job now, pay your expenses and save for tuition!" Conventional wisdom is valid - it knows and sees to it that the realities of life are handled now. If what you want is a *conventional life*, you should heed conventional wisdom. If you do not care about finding work you truly love, doing what you really want to do, follow the conventional wisdom.

For many students, an internship is simply the next step in an unorthodox life. If you had obeyed conventional wisdom you wouldn't be in college at all. Lack of money, good access to good high schools, little family support and your own family responsibilities could easily have prevented you from entering and sticking with college. The same energy that has brought you this far can take you past the financial obstacles of an internship. You can create a truly fulfilling future.

Self-test: Can I Afford To Intern?

Read these statements and put a checkmark by the ones that *honestly* apply to you.

____ I have a written budget that I strictly adhere to.

____ I shop for and cook all my meals, which are not on the school food plan.

____ I rarely purchase snacks or eat out.

____ I wear my clothes and shoes until they wear out, only then do I buy new items.

____ I do my own hair and nails and spend almost nothing on cosmetics.

____ I never purchase CDs, DVDs, videos, electronic games or books for leisure reading.

____ I enjoy entertainment and socializing almost exclusively at free events on campus.

____ I already work an evening or weekend job.

If you were not able to check most of these questions, there's room for you to adjust your lifestyle to make the sacrifice to take an internship. It will be challenging. But, like all delayed gratification, the rewards are worth it.

Making It Happen

In addition to sacrifice, creativity is the key to addressing the dilemma of the unpaid internship vs. the paid summer gig. If you are interested in going into a particular field and you simply must earn money and cannot land a paying internship, *look for low-level work in the field.*

Tiffany is a junior at Howard University and hopes one day to be a district attorney. She lives at home with her mother and brother in Washington, D.C . Taking a summer internship does not feel fair to her mother, who is facing the expenses of Tiffany's brother starting his freshman year of college in August. Balancing concern for her mother and brother and the hard reality that only those with some legal experience are even considered for her dream job, Tiffany decided to take a minimum wage file clerk job with a law firm.

Her responsibilities were to find files, file documents and word-process letters and forms, but from the first day Tiffany acted like she was assisting the attorneys. The secretarial workload was heavy, but she worked hard and smart to quickly finish her assigned duties, and got to know the associates and partners personally, asking them questions about the documents and their cases. They enjoyed her interest and soon began to pass the filing to other secretaries and gave Tiffany duties usually reserved for the interns and clerks.

If you need to earn and aren't able to get even a low-level job in your field of dreams, *make the most of the summer job you get.* For instance, you are working at the Cinnabon or Cineplex, but you have set your sights on finance and dream of being a CPA. Ask your supervisor if you can work with her on her accounting projects for no extra hourly pay, or on your day off, if you can help out in the regional office with the accounting books.

Lucas wanted to be a sports reporter, but he was broke and did not have family to support him. He got a job washing the news vans and trucks at local television station. The job was in the maintenance department, not the news department. Sometimes he even felt a little jealous and depressed watching interns his age go out on real stories while he was treated like a janitor. It was hot and not much fun, but it did give him a chance to chat with the photographers and reporters as they loaded their equipment into the vehicles.

The main sports anchor was impressed by Lucas' determination and offered him a non-paid job collecting high school football scores on Friday nights. That job turned into more unpaid work. Four months later, he was offered a studio crew position, which allowed him to learn even more about sports and broadcasting. In addition, he made valuable professional contacts that have benefited him in countless ways.

Look for volunteer opportunities right where you and your friends and family live, worship, and play. Whether your dream is to be a singer, chef or CEO, look for ways to practice your skills in organizations you know, especially small businesses and non-profits.

Yolonda, whose story opened this chapter, started interning and doing volunteer work when she was 16 and still in high school.

Volunteer service can satisfy three functions:
- You can do something for someone else and make a positive contribution to your community.
- Volunteer work will look good on your resume and your college application. It is not unusual for a good solid B student with voluntary community service to be accepted over an A student with little or no community service experience.
- If you treat your volunteer positions as though they are internships, you will gain experience and learn from the leaders of the organization. The key is to take advantage of every opportunity to learn new skills and perfect previously acquired ones.

Finally, you never know . . . *an unpaid internship can turn into cash.* Olga took an unpaid internship in music - an area about which she is passionate - promoting a music website. She had to work another job part-time to pay her bills. Her work schedule was long, many of the hours were tedious, but she told herself, "It will just be for a season and the end is in sight." Her purpose sustained her, for she knew the opportunity to get experience in the online music business was rare. Although the internship was advertised as unpaid, one of her first out-of-office assignments paid $100 a day for the weekend. She earned an unexpected $200 and had the experience of her life!

Elisha was very clear about her desire to work in accounting, and worked hard at a local firm as an unpaid intern for two semesters. At the end of the second semester she was offered a job.

If you know the career you want or just think you'd like to pursue it, the sooner you start looking for internships in that field, the better.

Look for Perks

Unpaid does not always mean, "We will provide you absolutely no compensation." When you read the internship description, look for key phrases like *small stipend, transportation* (depending on the city that can be significant), or *lunch.* For example, below is a listing posted by the Kaufman Center on Idealist.org for interns interested in public relations, advertising or website development. Notice what they offer instead of money.

"Requirements: This is an UNPAID internship, but Interns making a minimum commitment of 20 hours per week will have the opportunity to attend free classes and Merkin Concert Hall performances, as tickets are available. A public transportation stipend is also offered."

Suddenly, unpaid looks doable!

Win-Win-Win

When you land a career - launching internship, everybody wins. The corporations gain access to talented diverse students, the students gain valuable work experience that will prepare them for the 'real world', the universities gain knowledge from the valuable experiences the students bring back to share with their peers. Now that you know why you should intern, let's look at ways to get started!

SURVIVAL STRATEGIES FOR LIVING ON UNPAID INTERNSHIPS

You CAN work in an unpaid internship and still have income and a good time. Keep the big picture in mind. You are going somewhere. A vision of the bigger picture makes the sacrifices make sense.

- **Find a part time, evening or night job.** Tell everyone you know that you are looking for part time, off-hours work and then tell people you don't know. Try conventional avenues, such as temporary agencies.
- **House sit.** Scour websites and newspapers for people who need someone to take care of their home or apartment while they are away in exchange for living there for free.
- Pack your lunch **Walk or bike or carpool.** Vanessa's internship was in a two-fare zone from where she was rooming with a family friend (for free!). In order to save the extra fare, she walked the two miles rather than taking the bus. By the end of the summer she had lost those 15 freshman/ sophomore pounds she had put on since high school. A bonus!
- Pack your lunch rather than buy it.
- Hang out differently. Host a pot luck where everyone brings a dish, for example, rent a movie and pop your own popcorn.
- Choose your friends wisely. Avoid hanging with the superficial and pretentious friends who want to buy designer clothes and press you to do so. Rather, hang out with people who have similar interests. They'll understand why you have no money and why you find it worth the sacrifice.
- Discover FREE things, from "no cover, no minimum" times at clubs to computer labs at the free public library. Public libraries are havens for students who are on a budget.

2

YOUR INTERNSHIP SEARCH BEGINS

Your search begins when you start to identify what makes you tick, what excites you. Pay attention to your passions in life. For example, if you love to dress, and often find yourself giving insightful advice on fashion, maybe you should consider a career in the fashion industry. If you don't know or have a lot of interests, consider an assessment like *Strongs Interest Inventory* or the *Self-Directed Search.* Assessments don't tell you what to do, but they can help you narrow down career paths and the work environment that aligns with your temperament, personality type, interests, abilities and values.) Your university career services department should be able to provide an assessment. You can also find them on plenty of websites. Just stick "Career Assessment Test" into any search engine and you'll be surprised at the variety to choose from.

Gaining Experience at Different Levels

If you're in high school, get volunteer experience in the area you are considering as a career. If the only work you have done has been baby sitting and you don't want to open a day care center or teach elementary school, you need to get into an environment that matches your interests. If you're interested in public policy or political science, volunteer in the office of your local assemblyman. You could discover that politics is not your cup of tea, or the experience could light a political fire in you and confirm your desire to purse a career in government.

If you're in college and have not made a career choice, let yourself fantasize. Jot down your the activities you like. Say, for example, you enjoyed your classes in political science and public policy. The reading assignments and the professor's lectures appealed to your desire to see justice done. You imagine a life where you make a difference. You recall the time when you were in junior high and participated in an outreach program to the poor by working in a soup kitchen. Now that you have more understanding about how "the system" works, you want to do more. Start by asking your professor about internships available in public service. Yes, you will have to ask people for help. That's the first and most important step. Who you know and who knows you matters, but what you do with this support matters more.

Remember Yolonda from the beginning of Chapter 1? She got her internship with a sports team through a connection she had at her church.

There are many resources at your disposal, probably more than you realize. The first thing you do is tell everyone you know that you are looking for an internship and be specific about what you want. When Olga (the young lady who landed the music Internet internship) asked about internships, she already knew that she wanted to work in music. She started with her music professor. Her conversation with him is an example of what to say.

Sample dialogue/telephone script:

"Professor Graham, taking your class has made me realize that I have a passion for music. I am not sure that I want to be a performer, but I know I want to do something in the Arts. I was wondering if you could suggest some contacts or places for me to look for internship opportunities this summer."

"Sure. Let's set up time and we can talk in my office."

"That would be great. I appreciate that. How about Thursday at 4pm?"

Take that conversation, mold it to your situation and match it to the people in your life—Mom, Dad, Uncle, Pastor, Professor,

Alumni of the University and friends. All these people need to know two things:
1. You are looking for an internship
2. What kind of internship you want.

You do this because you don't know who knows whom. You may think that your family isn't well connected, but when you start asking around, you will be astonished at the connections you can make. If you have a fear of asking for favors and engaging people in conversation, it helps to realize that people - even strangers- want to help and contribute to someone's future. Here's how you might talk with a total stranger about an internship.

Sample dialogue/telephone script

"I love animals and would like to volunteer here at the animal shelter. I am thinking about veterinary medicine as a profession and I know that I can get some good experience."

"Well, right now, we have all the volunteers we need."

"Oh. Well, can you recommend another shelter or animal hospital?"

"You know, if you had started back in January, you could have applied to the top animal hospital in town. They have an extensive summer program, but it is very competitive and it hardly pays if at all. April is too late to start, but I'm sure the shelters around town could use your help. You could go to the ASPCA, but go in person. They never answer the phone or return voicemail messages."

"Thanks for the lead."

Not to do list: Your Search

- **Don't complain that you have to know someone to get an internship.** Look, who you know can really help you, but not having a large network of professionals working for you is no excuse.

- **Don't spend more time on myspace.com or MTV.com than job sites. The Internet is a great place to start your search.** Here are some suggestions: www.monster.com; www.careerbuilders.com, www.idealist.org, www.blackcollegian.com, www.blackenterprise.com, www.businessweek.com, www.fortune.com and www.diversityinc.com
- **Don't pay for college services that you don't use.** Probably one of the most under-used places at your college is the career center. Make an appointment or go and visit the center and let the counselor know what you are looking for. They will be able to give you some guidance. After all, you are paying for this service as part of your tuition, whether you use it or not.
- **Don't think an internship will find you.** This is a search, so do some searching! Newspapers, magazines, books on internships are all resources. Also, get creative – make phone calls, attend job fairs, and offer to do unpaid work at companies you're interested in (even if they don't have an established internship   program.)

When to Search (The Early Bird . . .)

Time is what you need to obtain a quality internship. Shanice was waiting to hear from one company that had seemed promising for her first internship as a college student. It was April and she had not heard from them, so she opened the Yellow Pages and started cold calling public relation firms.

"Hello. My name is Shanice Bennett and I am a communications major at Virginia Tech. I am looking for an internship. I would like to send you my resume. To whom should I send it?"

She says she got a couple of interviews out of that strategy. Fortunately, the first company finally came through and it was a paid internship. It paid more than the places she had called, but she was not willing to wait.

"You have to be aggressive," says Shanice. "I wanted a plan B in case my first choice didn't come through."

The next year, she decided not to wait until April to nail something down. She had started in November on her own personal telephone campaign. She put together a list of 20 companies she was interested in. This time she said:

"Hi, my name is Shanice Bennett and I'm would like to intern with your company this summer. When is the best time to apply and to whom should I send my resume?"

Internship Calendar
(Highly Recommended for College Sophomores and above)

September   Begin search by asking professors, alumni, church, elected officials, family and friends for contacts

October   Search Internet, alumni directories, corporate directories of companies where you want to work, newspapers, trade journals, career centers

November   Write letters and submit applications and supporting documents

December   Before holidays, send follow-up letters and emails to confirm your applications are complete and you are being considered

January   Phone calls to follow up where you are being considered

February   Find unobtrusive ways to send application enhancers—your transcript if your GPA is exceptional, notice of any honors you've received or related experience you've gained since making the application

March   Receive notices of acceptance

Timeline Considerations

You cannot wait until April and think, "Oops what am I gonna do this summer?" and expect to find a good internship. By that time, the better internships are gone and internship programs at leading corporations have stopped accepting applications. They are already making their final decisions and the candidates can expect acceptance letters by mid-May, if not sooner.

Even though the positions are unpaid, you have to compete for the few positions available, and the earlier your application, the better your competitive position.

Another possible timeline for a paid internship at the company of your choice begins *this* summer for *next* summer. You should spend this summer researching companies to determine where you'd like to work and to get ready for the application process. Develop your writing samples and get them proof-read by someone whose editing skills you trust. Should your target company want an essay, you want to be ready.

The more prestigious a company, the more selective they can be, so you must make sure when you submit your application that it is COMPLETE. Just as your college application had multiple parts, your target company may have a multi-part application. Yours will end up in the trash can if it's not perfect.

Many of the major and influential companies have formal internship programs and are deluged with applications and resumes. Pay close attention because there are strict deadlines. Depending on the company, the application deadlines can be as early as November or December for that following summer. For example, the deadline for a summer internship application at *The New York Times* is November 15th. That is among the earliest deadlines (who wouldn't want to intern with an organization that has Pulitzer Prize winners on staff?), yet it illustrates the point. Start early.

Build Your Internship Team

In Chapter 1 and Chapter 2, you have read about students who took internships, both paid and unpaid. They were purposeful and had their career goals in mind. Some even turned what seemed like dead-end jobs into foundations for their futures.

You can do it, too, especially if you have a team. It is easy to become discouraged and give up on yourself. Ask yourself, "Who are five people I can enlist to hold me accountable to my plan to get an internship and help me discover how I can survive with an unpaid internship?" These people are folks you trust. Your list might include:

- *My toughest teacher or professor.*
- *My friend who understands that I want to get ahead more than I want to fit in with my peers.*
- *My pastor*
- *My guidance counselor at school.*

Tell your team members your goal. Write it down for them with a target date for each step. Your goal might read:

"I will get an internship that will help me learn more about human rights in three months. Since most internships in human rights are unpaid, I will also have to get a part-time job."

Some smaller goals to help you reach the larger goal might be:

- *I will write letters to three companies requesting information about internships by the end of next week."*
- *"I will go to five businesses everyday for the next four weeks to find a part-time job that will supplement my income."*

Give your team members permission to hold you accountable for the goals and target dates. Each one will ask you periodically how you are progressing toward your goal. Holding you accountable means they may remind, nag, and show you consequences. Deal with it!

Also share with your team members your concerns about what might get in the way or keep you from achieving your goal. For example:

- *There aren't any good businesses in my neighborhood."*
- *My family needs me to work full time."*
- *My parent does not support me and often discourages me."*
- *I won't make enough to save for school if I work part time."*

Ask your team to help you see which skills you have that will help you achieve your goal. For example:

- *"I am confident when I speak with people."*
- *"I am a hard worker."*
- *"I learn fast."*
- *"I am creative."*

Discuss with your team how your life will be different once you achieve this goal. Write down ways your life would improve if you were to reach the goal.

- *"I will know more about . . ."*
- *"I will know that hard work and sacrifice pay off."*
- *"When things get tough, I know I can handle it!"*

Do you feel weird about sharing this stuff with your team? If so, pick a different team or change your attitude! You need a support system of people who want what is best for you. On your team you need people who want you to succeed and would be honored to help you reach your goals. Once you get the help you are asking for, follow up on any leads your support team gives you. Keep the big picture in mind because you are going somewhere!

Your Search: Putting It All Together

- Know your strengths! Get clarity on your interests and abilities. If you are not sure, speak with your school's career counselor about some of the assessments available such as the Gallup Strengths Finder assessment.

- Develop your prospective list of potential employers.
- Determine in which city you want to do an internship.
- Contact companies or organizations and ask about their internship program. (See chapter 3 for steps to perfecting your resume).
- Tell everyone you know that you are looking for an internship.
- Be prepared to communicate specifically.
  - "I'm looking to do an internship in research or finance."
  - "I need to get experience working in a lab or on the trading floor."
  - "I am looking for an internship in marketing."
- Make a list of people to contact.
- Talk to the Dean of your specialty area
- Contact Career Services at your university.

Go on line. Keyword: Internship

Looking Ahead

Next, you need a resume. You may have prepared one to apply for the job at Burger King or you may have submitted one with your college application. Neither of these will do when you apply for an internship. In the next chapter you'll learn how to prepare a professional resume.

PARENTS CORNER: 5 ANNOYING TRAITS THAT TRANSLATE INTO CAREER SUCCESS

1. Seems to be ignoring you. (FOR THE THIRD TIME! DON'T MAKE ME COME IN THERE AND TURN THAT COMPUTER OFF!!!!!)

Able to concentrate and focus intensely on an activity in which she has high interest.

2. Indicates you don't live up to his standards. (For example, cleans the counters before I have finished dinner.)

The desire and ability to maintain or create order.

3.Will read late into the night with a flashlight under the covers, but won't do his math homework.

Inclined toward language arts and skills. (A math tutor can help him learn just enough to get by.)

4. Chimes into every conversation.

Inclined toward verbal arts and skills.

5. Draws and doodles on everything.

Inclined toward visual arts and skills

Your young person may ignore you, say you are a sloppy housekeeper, talk too much, make horrible grades in math, crave attention or sit around reading or doodling. Consider what the behaviors could suggest about your youth's gifts and help him or her discover their talents and channel their interests. An internship can provide an opportunity to explore their abilities in a real world setting.

3

"NO-EXPERIENCE"
RESUMES AND COVER LETTERS

Marcus and Jennifer are both interested in the same internship in the newsroom of a local television station. Marcus has wanted to be a reporter since he was in grade school. In order to get experience, he has hosted a show at his college radio station, spent a summer interning at the local city newspaper, and has taken several broadcast journalism classes. Marcus has already fulfilled his college department's internship requirement. Still, he wants to intern at the television station because he knows it would be a great learning opportunity.

Jennifer has only taken one broadcast journalism class. She has never been inside a real newsroom and isn't even sure she wants to work in the field. She is only applying at the television station because she needs credits from an internship to graduate and she has heard that the newsroom requires interns to work just two shifts a week. Plus, it's close to her apartment so she figures she could walk there.

If you were the person in charge of hiring interns at the television station, who would you hire? Marcus, right? It seems like a no-brainer. After all, he has more prior experience and seems like he would benefit the most from the internship. Well, guess what? Jennifer got the job.

How is that possible? While it's true Jennifer wasn't all that serious about the internship, she is great at writing cover letters and she had a resume ready to go as soon as the internship was posted. Marcus was busy with school activities and waited until the day before the application deadline. He slapped together a resume and was so rushed, he forgot to spell-check his cover letter. Marcus was also over-confident. He assumed that his prior experience would get him the internship so he didn't think he really needed to spend much time selling himself. He believed his list of accomplishments would speak for itself. Big mistake!

In this chapter, we're going to look at how to write cover letters and resumes that will help you land a career launching internship! There are templates you can use for your own correspondence, sample cover letters and resumes, and of course, a *Not To Do List*. First, let's take a look at what Marcus should have known about the importance of resumes and cover letters.

Resumes

The main purpose of a cover letter and resume is to make the person in charge of hiring think that you are the perfect candidate for the job. You need to quickly explain the qualifications and characteristics you possess that make hiring you a great idea.

Start with building your resume. Your cover letter will build on the resume and serve as an introduction to it. It's never too soon to begin working on your resume. In fact, you should always have a resume ready to go. You never know when you'll see a job or internship ad that piques your interest.

The resume you write now will be very different than the resume you write ten years from now. By then, you will (hopefully) have a lot of great experience. However, if you have only ever held babysitting jobs and you want an internship in accounting, coming up with a resume that shows relevant experience will be nearly impossible. Therefore, you need to redirect your focus to your academic achievements and any relevant activities.

All internship resumes should include:
- **Identifying information:** This includes your name, address, telephone number, e-mail address.

- **Objective Statement:** In certain professional fields this is optional. However, well-worded objective statements give potential employers and immediate understanding of what type of job/internship you are seeking.
- **Education:** Give the names, cities, and states of the schools you have attended, as well as the degrees and diplomas you have received. You should also list your major and minor and relevant coursework.
- **Experience:** List your job title, name of the company, city, state, and dates of employment. Then list your job responsibilities and any outstanding accomplishments. Don't forget relevant volunteer work, research, and leadership positions. List jobs even if they do not relate to your chosen field – describe your responsibilities in a way that shows you have a strong work ethic and important skills.
- **Honors:** Briefly list any honors, awards, or scholarships you have received. This shows that you are accomplished, not to mention a hard worker and fast learner. Do not list every trophy you won in high school. Try to keep this section limited to your time spent in higher education, unless your high school achievement was a real jaw-dropper.
- **Be one page:** Later in your career, you may find that your resume is two pages. However, internship resumes should only be one page. Unless you are the very rare exception, you have limited relevant experience. Don't make a hiring manager wade through a list of every badge you received in Boy Scouts or all of the classes you've taken since entering college. Less is more!

Resume Template

Here is a basic, solid resume template that you can use. Just fill in your own information and you are good to go!

Resume of [Full Name]
[Address, City, State, Zip] [Phone #] [Email Address]

Objective   One concise sentence here.

Experience   <Job Title>
<Company Name, City, State>
<Start Date> to < End Date>
<Optional Short Description>
- Job responsibility and/or achievement
- Job responsibility and/or achievement
- Job responsibility and/or achievement

<Job Title>
<Company Name, City, State>
<Start Date> to < End Date>
<Optional Short Description>
- Job responsibility and/or achievement
- Job responsibility and/or achievement
- Job responsibility and/or achievement

Education   If your education is more impressive than your experience, put this section before Experience.

<School Name, City State>
<Degree Earned, or Expected Date of Graduation>
<Major, (GPA if it is high)>
<Award, accomplishment, curricular activity, major /minor, relevant coursework>
<Award, accomplishment, curricular activity, major /minor, relevant coursework>

Honors/   This is an optional section. List any awards, achievements such as for military experience, special skills, or interests.

Activities   optional
optional
optional

References   Available upon Request

Sample Resume

ANGELA WASHINGTON
Ang.washington@gmail.com
(555) 555 - 5555

School Address	**Permanent Address**
Clarkson University	123 Riverside Road
235 South Avenue	Apartment B-3
Cleveland, OH 57487	Dayton, OH 51216

Objective: Seeking an internship in the banking/ finance industry.

Experience

ABC Company   New York, NY
Sales & Trading Summer Analyst
June 2006 – Aug 2006
- Rotated through various equity, fixed income and foreign exchange desks
- Researched and presented a comprehensive review of the Equity Prime Brokerage desk that included initiatives for future growth

XYZ Corporation   Brooklyn, NY
Account Executive Intern
June 2005 – Aug 2005
- Successfully completed six module training course and gained an   in depth understanding of the consumer lending and real estate industries
- Initiated the loan approval process for client applications and generated daily reports on application status
- Responsible for daily audit and processing of client payments

123 Corporation   New York, NY
Sales Supervisor
Oct 2000 – Feb 2003
- Managed 5 members of the Sales Department
- Responsible for producing monthly budgets and reports for senior management
- Generated invoices, quotations and purchase orders and improved sales by over 30%

Education
    Clarkson University, Cleveland, OH
    Bachelor of Science in Business Economics with a minor in Mathematics
    Graduation Date: May 2008   *Cumulative GPA:* 3.9

Relevant Coursework:
Money & Banking	Advanced Corporate Finance
Financial Management	Financial Accounting
Macroeconomics	Econometrics
Microeconomics	Statistics I & II
International Financial Management	

Leadership
    Clarkson University, Cleveland, OH   Cleveland, OH
    Tutor   Oct 2004 – Present
    • Identified students' weaknesses and aided them in comprehending
      challenging mathematical concepts and reasoning
    • Developed a computerized database of student information to enable
      weekly reports to be generated

    Clarkson University Student Leaders Cleveland, OH
    Orientation Leader   May 2004 – Present
    • Mentored group of thirty new students
    • Led campus tours and ensured students' participation in orientation
      week events

Honors & Awards
    • Full Presidential Scholarship
    • Honors Program

Skills
Proficient in Microsoft Office Suite, working knowledge of UVX
financial software

Sample Resume

Jamie Williams
123 Main Street
Mytown, CA 39383
(222) 222-2222
jamiew@email.com

OBJECTIVE: Seeking an internship in sales and marketing.

EDUCATION: California State College
Sunnyside, CA
Bachelor of Business Administration
May 2008
Major: Marketing
GPA: 3.5
Honors: Deans List, Honor Society

EXPERIENCE:

Spring 2006   Major Record Label   Mytown, CA
STUDENT INTERN/GROUP COORDINATOR
- Collaborated with teammates to accomplish goals
- Created three new school events to promote recording artists
- Oversaw all functions and operations of group members

Summer 2005   YMCA   Mytown, CA
MARKETING ASSISTANT
- Implemented marketing plans to promote center events
- Organized activities to increase membership
- Created incentives to promote health and wellness

Summer 2004   Downtown Medical Office   Mytonw, CA
SECRETARY/ASSISTANT
- Maintained account log of daily transactions
- Organized insurance information
- Calculated final patient expenses

HONORS &
ACTIVITIES: Student Government Association
Alpha Lambda Delta Honor Society
Sophomore Class President
American Marketing Association
Junior Class Treasurer
Big Brother/Big Sisters Program

SKILLS: WordPerfect, Microsoft Power Point,
Excel, Internet

REFERENCES: Available upon request.

Convincing Cover Letters

For one moment, put yourself in the shoes of a manager in charge of hiring an intern. You only need to hire one intern and you want to make it quick and painless. Let's face it, you have more pressing responsibilities, including overseeing your *paid* employees. In front of you sits a stack of 50 resumes and cover letters. How do you pick one? What will separate the successful applicant from those who will get the "Thanks, but no thanks." response letter. Something in one of the cover letters needs to stand out to catch your attention.

Now, let's pretend you are a potential intern who has sent one of the envelopes in that stack. What makes you think that you will be the one to get the job? As Marcus and Jennifer have proven, it is not your qualifications alone that will win you the internship. It is how you sell your qualifications. And you better make it fast! The average hiring manager only gives a cover letter a few seconds before forming an impression of the candidate.

Whether you mail or email your cover letter, it should make the prospective employer want to pick up the phone and call you immediately. It is important to use upbeat language that shows you have the energy and passion necessary for the position; just keep it professional. No gushing on and on about how you could "do a really super job." Don't just say you would be great – prove it with an example. If you want a position in a lab, don't say, "I am detail-oriented." Instead, say something like, "Three semesters in the University's chemistry lab has taught me the value of meticulous work. As a result, I am extremely detail oriented and committed to precise methodology."

Finally, make sure your cover letter and resume are PERFECT. No typos, no grammatical mistakes. Use spell check and proofread several times. Once you think it is error free, give it to someone else to read. A second pair of eyes will often pick up any mistakes you missed.

"Not to do" List – Correspondence Mistakes

- **Don't send the same cover letter to everyone.** Tailor each letter according to the specific position. Hiring managers can tell if you've taken the time to write a unique letter or have simply printed off a "one size fits all" form letter.

- **Don't forget to check for mistakes.** We've already covered this, but it is crucial. Typos and spelling errors make you look sloppy and careless. I've received cover letters where applicants have spelled my name or company wrong. Even worse, I've received letters addressed to someone else (they obviously didn't take the time to change the name on their standard form letter before mailing it to me).

- **Don't sound like a robot.** It's important to show some personality in your letter. Carefully pick words that best describe your most impressive qualities.

- **Don't be too casual.** Showing your personality does not mean it is okay to write a cover letter that sounds like a note to your best friend. Keep it professional.

- **Don't send a resume without a cover letter.** Your cover letter is an important introduction that explains why you are sending your resume. A potential employer should never have to ask what position you are applying for. Plus, if you can't take the time to write a cover letter, how much can you really want the internship?

- **Don't ignore blatant requests.** If the employer has written, "No Phone Calls" in the job posting, don't end your cover letter by saying, "I'll call you next week to set up an interview."

Cover Letter Template

Here is a good template to follow whenever you need help writing a cover letter.

Your Name
Your Address
Your City, State, Zip Code
Your Phone Number
Your Email
Date

Name
Title/Organization
Address
City, State, Zip Code

Dear Mr./Ms. Last Name:

First Paragraph: Briefly explain why you are writing this letter. Include the name and title of the position you are interested in and how you heard about the position. If you have a mutual contact or friend, mention it here. Do not make this paragraph any longer than a few sentences.

Next Paragraph: Now it's time to sell yourself. Explain your qualifications and what makes you a good fit for the position. Do not give your entire resume. Instead, make a few statements about why your abilities match what they are looking for and give examples. Don't forget to include whatever it is that makes you unique, including your education, experience, awards, volunteer service, or anything else that is relevant to the position. Feel free to refer the reader to important information contained in your resume, "As you will see from my resume..."

Conclusion Paragraph: Mention that you would be happy to provide more information.Such as work references, writing samples or your most recent college transcripts. State how you will follow up on this letter and indicate when you will do so. For instance, say "I will give you a call later next week..." Make sure you thank them for their time and/or consideration and mention that you look forward to hearing from them.

Sincerely,
Your Signature
Your Typed Name

Sample Internship Cover Letter –
Public Relations

John Belden
123 E. Market St.
Mytown, NY 12345
555-555-5555

February 12, 2007

Ms. Marge Hacken
Public Relations Manager
ABC Industries
456 South Street
Yourtown, NY 67890

Dear Ms. Hacken,

I am writing to express my interest in the public relations summer internship position. After reviewing my resume, Ms. Rene Holtz from Ohio State University's career service office suggested I contact you. I am currently a junior and plan to receive a B.A. in Public Relations in May, 2008.

I have gained valuable public relations experience, both in my college coursework and through real world experience. Last year, I wrote three successful press releases for events held by the campus International Club. My efforts helped our club receive coverage in the student newspaper, The Lantern and on WOSR 91.1. I also volunteered as a media liaison during the 2003 and 2004 Breast Cancer Walk For A Cure in Columbus. Additionally, I have served as the Chapter President and Treasurer of the Public Relations Student Society of America.

I am certain that my existing experience, coupled with my desire to learn and great attitude will make me a valuable member of your public relations intern team. I will call you next week to see if we can schedule an interview. In the meantime, please feel free to contact me at (555) 5555-555 or through email at jbelden@myemail.com. Thank you for your consideration.

Sincerely,

John Beldon
John Beldon

Sample Internship Cover Letter – Sales

Lucy Lawson
123 E. Market St.
Mytown, NY 12345
555-555-5555

February 12, 2007

Mr. Miles Alexander
Universal Orlando
1000 Universal Studios Plaza
Orlando, Florida 32819

Dear Mr. Alexander,

I am extremely interested in your request for a sales intern. Your ad posting in the Monrovian University career services office caught my eye because I believe my outgoing personality, desire to learn, and work experience make me an excellent candidate for the position.

For the last three years, I have coordinated ticket sales for the annual Goodwill Gala held at Monrovian University. As you can see from my resume, I also have a proven track record of success in retail sales. Moreover, I have taken three marketing courses in the last year that have better prepared me for an internship within with your organization.

I am a big fan of Universal Orlando and welcome the opportunity to bring my enthusiasm and commitment to your sales department. I will call you in one week to arrange an interview. Should you want to contact me before that time, you may reach me via phone or via email (lucyl@myemail.com). Thank you for your consideration.

Sincerely,
Lucy Lawson
Lucy Lawson

Sample Email Internship Cover Letter – Engineering

Subject Line of Email Message: Engineering Internship Position

Email Message:

Dear Hiring Manager,
I am extremely interested in your website job posting for engineering interns. In talking with some of your past interns, I have learned that your firm has a strong commitment to education. I am confident that your values and objectives would compliment my own goals, enthusiasm, and work ethic.

During my three years at Indiana State, I have prepared for this type of internship by:

- Completing a cooperative experience with XYZ Engineering, where I helped collect data for highway improvement project
- Taking coursework in soil mechanics, foundation formation, and structural analysis
- Helping conduct a university survey of traffic flow on the campus' main thoroughfare

Additionally, I posses strong mathematical and communication skills. As my professors and past employers can attest, I am conscientious and reliable. My resume, which is below, provides more information on my experience and qualifications. Should you require references, I would be happy to provide the names and contact information of the people who have directly supervised my work. I look forward to hearing from you as soon as possible to arrange time for an interview. Thank you for your consideration.

Sincerely,

Amanda Jones
Ajones@myemail.edu

4

FROM PHONE CALLS TO INTERVIEWS - MAKING A GOOD FIRST IMPRESSION

"I wish I had a camera in my office so I could show you the parade of inappropriate outfits that have come through the door," says Marlene Hachet, human resource manager of a major company. "There are so many young people their 20s who come here in trendy outfits. They look like they are going to a club, not a job interview!"

Marlene says she has seen it all. "I've interviewed girls in mini skirts and flip flops and guys with pants hanging off their butt and big diamond stud earrings. I don't know if they would have been good interns - because as soon as I saw their outfits, I didn't seriously consider them for the job. Their outfits told me they were not ready to be a professional."

Ouch! It seems a little harsh, but it's a cold reality. We are all judged by the way we dress and carry ourselves. Internships are very competitive. In some cases, hundreds of people will apply for the same opening. If you are lucky enough to get an interview, don't blow it by choosing the wrong outfit.

Remember, you only have one chance to make a good first impression, whether you are talking to someone on the phone or shaking their hand. In this chapter, we are going to concentrate on making those first impressions positive. We are going to take a look at how to set-up an interview, prepare for the big day, and then interview with confidence.

Speaking Well When Speaking Matters

You've sent your resume and cover letter but you haven't heard anything. It's been nearly two weeks and now it is time to make the call. Do you just pick up the phone, call the company's main number, and start stammering about needing to check if your envelope got there? Sure, if you want to sound like a blathering idiot.

Let's take a step back and look at what you need to do before you dial. First, always make sure that you have the right information. You need to know the name of the person you are trying to reach and their job title. Now check your watch. Is it a good time to call? Are you in the same time zone as the person you are calling? If not, what time is it there? Are you sure their office is open? Is it lunchtime? If you call midday, you will have less of a chance of getting a hold of the person you need to reach.

Quite often we hear from students who say, "I tried calling, but I didn't have the right information." That's not a valid excuse. There are many ways to find out contact information, including your career services office and the Internet.

Okay, now that you have the right contact information, take a few moments to plan exactly what you are going to say. It's a good idea to write a little script that you can refer to in case you get nervous.

Sample Telephone dialogue:

"Good afternoon, may I speak to Ms. Deidre Brown please. This is Thomas Stewart."

"One moment," says the receptionist.

(The phone rings and someone picks up.)

"This is Deidre."

"Hello Ms. Brown. My name is Thomas Stewart. I sent you my resume and cover letter for the internship position in your office last week, which I am hoping you have received. I'm very excited about the opportunity and want to follow up with you to make sure I can be considered for the position."

When you call to inquire about an internship or job, keep the following in mind:

- Sound pleasant, Not demanding!
- Be brief because the person you are speaking to probably does not have a lot of time.
- Know the details, such as when you sent your resume, the name and title of the person to whom you sent it, and the position you are applying for.
- Offer to send any additional information they might require.
- Quickly reiterate your interest in the position.
- Be extremely polite and thank them for taking the time to speak with you.

They've Called You Back... Now What?

Not long ago, I called a young man to interview him for a position. Like always, I asked him if I was calling at a good time. He said it was, so I proceeded to ask a few questions. He sounded distracted and kept saying, "Excuse me, what did you say?" After a few minutes of a frustrating conversation, I heard a car horn honk.

I said, "Are you driving right now?"

He replied, "Yeah. I'm going over a bridge and traffic is pretty heavy."

"Why don't you call me back when you can speak to me without putting your life in jeopardy," I said.

I would like to say this was an isolated incident, but this happens all of the time. My colleagues have all complained about students making this mistake. Do everyone a favor and don't pick up your phone if you are in a room filled with people, if there is loud music in the background, if you at the gym working out, or in class. Take it from me, people would rather get your voicemail and talk to you at a later time than talk to you while you are distracted and can not conduct a professional conversation. If you do answer the phone and it is a bad time, simply say, "I'm very glad you called, but this is not a good time. May I call you back?" Then, get their name, number, and the best time to reach them.

How you answer your phone and the message you place on your voicemail is also important. Don't ever pick up the phone and say, "Yeah. Who's this?" if you have ever given out a particular phone number as your business contact number. You need to be professional at all times when answering your phone. You never know who is on the other end of the line. Your voicemail should also be very simple, pleasant and professional. Go with the standard:

"Hello, this is Brent. Please leave your name, number, and the best time to reach you and I will return your call as soon as possible."

That's it! No gimmicks, no jokes, no loud music.

Not long ago, I was talking to a woman who needed to hire three interns for a great summer position at a travel magazine. It was a fantastic internship and she had dozens of impressive applicants to choose from. She narrowed down her selection based on the resumes and cover letters she received and then started placing phone calls to set up interviews.

Here's how her conversation went:

"Hello, this is Tyra Craig," she said, "Is James Martin there?"

"He don't live here anymore!" said a voice that sounded very irritated.

"Oh. I'm sorry," she said. "I'm calling about a resume he sent me. Do you know how to reach him?"

"How should I know? I'm his mother, not his answering service." Click.

Needless to say, James Martin did not even get an interview, let alone the job. Let this story be a warning to you. If you give a phone number that belongs to your parents or anyone else, make sure they know that someone may call them. Ask them to be polite and take a message. If you have any reason to believe that they will be rude or not give you the message, do not put their number on your correspondence. You can't risk having someone else make a bad first impression before you even get a chance to say "hello."

Talking While.... (Urban, Young, Surfer Dude, Valley Girl, or Whatever)

We all have accents. It is part of who we are and where we come from. However, if you have an accent that is difficult for some people to understand or you speak in an overly casual way using too much slang, you need to change it – fast!

How you speak is just as important as how you dress. It doesn't matter if you are wearing the most conservative suit in the world, if you open your mouth and sound like a surfer dude, mall chick, or street thug you probably will not get the internship or job. When you are talking to a potential employer, he or she is not just judging what you say, but also how you say it.

Save the slang for your friends. Never use it in an interview. Slang is not polished or professional. Even worse, the interviewer might not be as cool as you are so they may not understand what you are saying! Also, it goes without saying that you should never swear or use profanity during an interview.

Even if slang is not a problem for you, you may find yourself saying things like, "ummmm," "uhhh," or "ya know" when you are trying to think of the next thing to say. These so-called "verbal fillers" can make you sound unpolished and unprofessional.

The good news is that you can learn to speak in a way that will make you fit into corporate culture. You just have to practice, practice, practice.

Here are some ideas to get you started:

- Check out your college's career service center. They should be able to provide coaching and mock interviews.
- Find a professor or mentor who is willing to take the time to speak to you and correct you as you go.
- Read the newspaper aloud everyday. This can also help you build your vocabulary. Keep a dictionary nearby and look up any words with which you are unfamiliar.

- Join a group like Toastmasters or a debating team. Some of the most well spoken students we see at the Thurgood Marshall College Fund are members of Toastmasters.
- Take a public speaking class. All universities offer them and many even require them.
- Speak like a professional all the time. You don't need to use 50 cent words when you are talking to your friends, but try to start speaking clearly and eloquently on a consistent basis.

Remember, speaking well is not like a test you can cram for the night before! You have to constantly work at it. When you are stressed during an interview, the last thing you want to have to concentrate on is your speech. Professional speech should become second nature to you.

Preparing for the Interview

It pays to be prepared for the interview. Be ready to explain all of the information you have provided on your resume. Come up with short, but informative answers to the most common interview questions, including:

- Tell me about yourself. (This is an opportunity to briefly tell where you are from, the schools you have attended, work history, and your career aspirations. Keep it positive, interesting, and fairly short!)
- Why do you want to work here?
- Tell me about an experience with a difficult situation on the job and how you handled it.
- What do you like about this field?
- What are some of your strengths and weaknesses?
- What do you hope to get out of this internship?
- Why do you think you would be a good fit for this position?

As I've mentioned already, mock interviews are a terrific way to practice. Not only will they give you a chance to develop your professional speaking voice, you will get a chance to think of solid answers that you can deliver smoothly and confidently.

Self Test – Getting Ready For the Interview

A few days before an interview, take this test. Use it as a checklist to make sure you are ready.

_____ Do you have all of the printed materials you will need, including a copy of the resume you sent to the company, references, and the job description?

_____ Are your materials in a professional and neat folder or briefcase?

_____ Is your clothing professional? Is it pressed and clean?

Business attire is almost always correct for any interview. It is perfectly acceptable to be more conservatively dressed than your interviewer: you interviewer already has a job! Gentleman should always wear a suit and tie. Ladies should invest in an interview suit as well, but often dress slacks or a skirt and blouse combination will be sufficient.

- Are your shoes clean and professional? Remember, no scuffs and no sneakers! High heels are only appropriate if you can walk in them.
- What jewelry will you wear, if any? Women should stay away from anything too large or trendy. Men should try to avoid jewelry as much as possible. Better to be too conservative than too flashy.

Burned by Myspace.com

This is a problem that didn't even exist until recently. Before the Internet became part of everyday life, it was much easier to keep your professional and personal life separate. However, that's no longer the case. If you appear on any questionable websites, remove your pictures and identifying information before you send out your resume. Also check the email address you use to contact potential employers. If it is partyanimal@aol.com, sexygirl@yahoo.com, or beerguzzler@msn.com, you better change it to something more appropriate.

Recently, I heard about a hiring manager who canceled an interview with a young woman who seemed perfect on paper. Unfortunately, for the young woman, the hiring manager "Googled" her, meaning she put the candidate's name in the popular Internet search engine. Suddenly, there she was, posing in inappropriate photos with some friends. The content of the website also contained several racial slurs. That young woman still doesn't really know why she didn't get the interview.

I've talked to potential employers who have been turned off by comments they've read on a young person's myspace.com page. If you are posting things like blogs where you trash-talk your current employer or are posing for questionable pictures, you are playing with fire. The internet is public and is accessible to your prospective employer as well as your friends.

It's Interview Time!

You've arrived on time and are waiting in the lobby for the interviewer to arrive. You're nervous. Now what?

First relax! Take a few deep breaths. You want to appear calm and confident. If you have prepared for this interview, you have nothing to worry about.

Greet the interviewer with a warm smile and a firm handshake. Don't forget to look him/her in the eye.

When you are offered a seat, say "Thank you." Then sit up straight and keep a pleasant look on your face. Remember the eye contact and plenty of smiles.

When speaking, make sure the interviewer can hear your voice. No mumbling. Your want to sound fully engaged in the conversation, not monotone or unenthusiastic. It's perfectly okay to take a moment to think about a question. You don't need to rush. Also, give the interviewer time to get out each question. Don't interrupt them, and if you do, immediately apologize and give them a chance to continue.

During the interview, let the interviewer be your guide. Follow their cues to see what behavior is appropriate. However, never be too casual in your speech, even if they are "letting it all hang out." You still need to look professional. When you are asked a question, keep your responses specific. Don't ramble and ask for clarification if you think you do not understand the question.

Sometimes you may find yourself with an interviewer who likes small talk but never asks you about your strengths. Be prepared to take the initiative and give a few examples of your accomplishments.

Also be prepared to ask questions to increase your understanding of the company and position you want. If you can't think of anything to ask, consider a few of the following:

How much supervision will I receive and who will be supervising me?

- What qualities are you looking for in a candidate?
- Is there any travel involved in the position?
- When do you expect to make a hiring decision?
- What are the hours I would work?
- How many interns do you hire in a year?

You should also go to the interview knowing basic information about the company, such as what it produces, how long it is been around, and who the CEO is. Most companies will have a website with this information posted on it. Don't be caught looking like you didn't care enough to take an interest in the organization.

"Not to do" List - What NOT to do during an Interview

- **Don't forget to know something about the company.** As I just stated in the last section, find out what you can about the organization before your interview. It will show that you have done your homework and are serious about theinternship. Having a few facts about the company at which you hope to intern will also give you something to talk about during the interview.

- **Don't dress inappropriately.** Check your appearance before you leave for the interview. Are your fingernails clean? How is your hair? Is your outfit professional, clean and pressed, not too casual or trendy?

- **Don't show up late.** Give yourself plenty of time to get there. Allow extra time for traffic and/or bad directions.

- **Don't bring a friend, your mom, your boyfriend or girlfriend.** You would be surprised at how many people bring friends, relatives, significant others, or parents to an interview. If you have to have someone go with you for instance, because they are giving you a ride, do not let them wait on the premises. Suggest they drop you off and come back when it is time to pick you up. Don't even allow them to wait in the lobby. What if your interviewer walks you out at the end of the meeting? Do you want him or her to see your mom waiting for you? You must look like an independent professional.

What's Next?

The interview went well. Now what?

Immediately follow-up with a personalized thank you card or letter. Send it within 24 to 48 hours of the interview. It is okay to send a "thank you" email, but still plan to send a letter.

A thank-you letter is another opportunity to sell yourself. But it is not another cover letter. Your thank you letter shows that you are courteous and professional. It also gives you an important chance to reiterate why you think you are a great candidate and confirm your interest in the position. It even gives you an advantage over your competition, who might not be savvy enough to send a thank you letter.

Many people are unsure if they should send a handwritten card or a formal letter. Both are appropriate, but I personally prefer the printed letter, especially if you do not have excellent handwriting. Your letter should appear short and professional. If you handwrite a letter, you may have to squeeze too much information on the card, making it look sloppy. With a typed letter, you can include much more information and still have it look brief.

Thank You Letter Template

Fill in your specific information.
Then stick it in the mail less than 48 hours after your interview.

Your Name
Street
City, State, Zip Code
Phone number
Email address

Today's Date

Interviewer's name/Title
Company Name
Street address
City, State, Zip code

Dear (interviewer's name):
Immediately thank them for taking the time to talk to you. (Make sure you mention the day you interviewed and the position for which you interviewed for. This paragraph should not be more than one or two sentences.)
In the second paragraph, indicate you interest in the job. Now that you know more about the position, here is your chance to further explain why you are the perfect candidate. Feel free to use bullet points here:
• Why you are qualified – be specific about your experience
• Another reason you'd be great at the job
• One more reason to hire you
In this optional paragraph, you can mention something that happened during the interview that was special. For instance, "I appreciate the tour you gave me of the plant. It certainly is an impressive production facility. Seeing your operation made me even more interested in learning more about your products and services."
This final paragraph should say thank you one more time. Offer to provide more information. Close by saying that you look forward to hearing from them again.

Sincerely,

[Sign here]
Your name

The Waiting Game

Waiting to find out if you got the internship can be tough! Don't freak out and start calling them everyday to ask if they have made a decision. Simply send your thank you letter and chill out.

Your interview was your opportunity to ask about the next step. You should have already asked when you could expect them to contact you. Do not call before then. If you do not hear from them during their timeframe, wait at least a few more days and then call. If you call too soon, it will look like you can't follow instructions. If you do not know when they are planning to get back to you, wait at least two weeks after the interview before you call.

When you do call, follow the same guidelines provided at the beginning of this chapter for setting up an interview. Prepare what you are going to say, be brief, and above all, polite.

If you call and are told that they do not want to hire you for the internship, thank them and tell them that you enjoyed the interviewing process. Also say that if they change their minds or have an additional opening in the future, you hope they keep you in mind. It is okay to ask why they chose another candidate over you, but only ask if you are sincerely looking for constructive advice. Remain polite, brief, and thank them for their explanation.

For as long as he can remember, Terrence has always wanted to work with exotic animals. As a young child, he used to tell everyone he was going to "train lions" for a living and "go to Africa to study gorillas." As he got a little older, he figured the best way to work with animals was to become a veterinarian. During his sophomore year as a biology major, one of his favorite instructors suggested Terrence explore internships at regional zoos. She explained that most vets don't come in contact with the exotic animals Terrence wanted to work with everyday. She thought he might be better off learning what it takes to become a zookeeper or researcher, since he seemed more excited about studying animal behavior and teaching the public about wildlife then performing medical procedures.

PARENTS CORNER: HELPING YOUR CHILD PREPARE FOR AN INTERVIEW

If you want to help you child ace an interview, read this chapter. It has a lot of good advice and will give you a basic idea of how your child should prepare.

Our career counselors at TMSF often deal with parents. Here is what they have to say about your role in the interview process:

- Be polite when taking phone calls and messages. Remember the person who calls you may be trying to give your child a job.
- Don't forget to give your child any important messages.
- Encourage role playing exercises. Interview your child and let him or her interview you.
- Consider taking your child to work with you to learn more about various careers and professional setting.
- If you provide financial support to your child, make sure they have a decent interview outfit, paper for resumes and other correspondence and materials. Many parents don't hesitate to buy their kids iPods or Air Jordans, but balk at shelling out money for a decent suit. Ask yourself which gifts are the most important. If you can't offer financial assistance, come up with ways to help your child prepare for an interview on a budget.
- Offer your opinion. If you see your daughter going to an interview in a micro-mini, pull her aside and say, "Look, that's not an appropriate outfit."
- Offer your proofreading skills. Volunteer to read your child's letters and resumes. An extra set of eyes is always a good idea!

5

NAVIGATING CORPORATE CULTURE

Her advice excited Terrence and he began investigating internships. Four months later, he landed a summer internship at one of the nation's top zoos. Terrence was one of three interns in the community relations department. All three had hoped to be spending a lot of time with the animals, but it didn't work out that way. They mostly answered phone calls and helped coordinate summer educational programs for children. Terrence was a little disappointed that he was stuck in an office, but he still worked hard everyday.

After about two weeks, the other two interns, Mark and Stacy, figured out the times that their manger was too busy to supervise them. They used those hours to surf the Internet or sit outside in the sun. While Terrence worked alone, Mark and Stacy had the nerve to complain that they were bored!

One afternoon their manager, Clem, returned from a meeting early and was surprised to find only Terrence sorting mail. Terrence didn't rat out Mark and Stacy, but it confirmed Clem's previous suspicions that they were slacking. After all, the guy wasn't stupid. He knew which intern was serious about contributing to the job.

Over the next two months, Terrence noticed that Clem often ignored Mark and Stacy. If there was a job that needed to be done, he called Terrence. While Terrence rarely got "up close and personal" with the animals, he ended up learning a lot about how zoos operate. Mark and Stacy didn't seem to care that Terrence was doing extra work. It just gave them more time to goof off. When the summer ended, Clem thanked Terrence for his efforts and promised to keep him in mind for future opportunities.

Three months later, Terrence received a phone call from Clem. The zoo was beginning exciting research on the reproductive physiology of the giant panda. Clem said he could get Terrence a spot on the spring internship team. Terrence immediately began reading as much as he could about pandas. Sure enough, Clem came through for him and Terrence spent the spring working on the project. That summer, he even traveled to the Chengdu Research Base for Giant Panda Breeding in China as part of the zoo's cultural exchange program.

"It was the best experience of my life," Terrence says. "I got three things out of it. First, I was able to live out my dream of seeing rare animals. Second, I also feel like I really did something important toward helping save them from extinction. Third, the trip to China and the research I've done since then has opened up a lot of doors professionally."

One month after returning home from Asia, Terrence ran into Mark at a party. Mark was amazed that the zoo had sent Terrence to China. He said, "That sucks! Why didn't Clem call me? Finally, they let the interns do something interesting and they don't let me know about it!" Terrence didn't bother to bring up the hot afternoons during the prior summer that he had spent alone sorting mail and answering the phones.

It is pretty obvious why Clem went out of his way to help Terrence after his first internship ended. Clem knew that his three interns weren't thrilled by their jobs, but he still expected them to be professional. Only Terrence maintained a positive attitude, completed assignments on time, and seemed eager to learn about all aspects of running a zoo. Terrance also showed initiative and was always eager to take on additional responsibilities. In short, he acted like a valued employee. Mark and Stacy acted like spoiled children.

"Not to do" List - What NOT to do during an Internship

Want to make a great impression during your internship and maybe even end up with a real job offer? If you do, then avoid every single thing on this "Not to do" list.

- **Don't arrive chronically late** – While none of us can help the occasional three car pile up or public transportation problem, arriving to the office late should not become routine.

- **Don't speak rudely to any member of the staff** – This goes from the CEO down to the maintenance workers. You never know who knows who. Don't assume stories of your rudeness won't circulate and hurt your reputation.

- **Don't decline offers to dine with your boss or management** – This is a networking opportunity and a chance to pick their brains, gain valuable insight and maybe even a professional mentor.

- **Don't conduct personal business at work** – This isn't the time to check your emails or make phone calls to friends and family.

- **Don't tell your supervisor what you can't or won't do** – If you are having difficulty with an assignment, ask for clarification or seek assistance from other employees in the department. Never say flat out that you just can't do something, especially if you haven't even tried first.

- **Don't blow off office functions that you are invited to** – Again this is a networking opportunity. You never know who you'll meet!

- **Don't forget to take your internship seriously** – Your internship is a break into a professional environment that other students would happily accept, so understand the importance of this opportunity.

- **Don't use poor grammar or slang** – Remember to use proper English at all times, no EBONICS. Always enunciate. If you have a heavy accent, it may be hard for others to understand you.

- **Don't forget to use basic etiquette** – Don't be the person people remember because you didn't cover your mouth when you coughed or you smacked your gum.
- **Don't forget to use proper dinning etiquette** - Be sure you are familiar with a formal table setting in case you are invited to corporate dining events. Make sure you know which fork and glass to use for different courses of the meal. Even in less formal dinning settings, always observe proper table manners.
- **Don't get drunk at corporate functions** – If liquor is being served, it does not give you free reign to get wasted. Don't drink at all. Your main focus should be networking. Remember, corporate functions may look like parties, but they are professional events.
- **Don't be anti-social during corporate functions.** – The purpose is to mingle and meet new people in the company. This is not the time to become a hermit.
- **Don't sit around doing nothing** – If you have completed your assignment, go back to your supervisor and ask if there is anything else you can do. Take initiative in seeking out new projects. Remember how working hard earned Terrence a trip to China?
- **Don't gossip about coworkers** – Talking about people or sharing a juicy story can be tempting, but don't do it! You never know who is listening.
- **Don't quit!** – Okay, you realize that this internship isn't exactly all you thought it would be. Don't give up. There are still valuable skills that you can gain from the experience. Quitting sends a very bad message to management. Even worse, you took an opportunity away from a student who really wanted it. You will also be hard pressed to get a letter of recommendation from a job that you quit. Don't burn your bridges!

Don't ever make the mistake of thinking, "This stuff doesn't matter. It's only an internship, not a real job." According to the

National Association of Colleges and Employers' 2004 Experiential Education Survey, the average employer offered full-time positions to more than half of the students who served in internships with their companies. Treat your internship like an extended job interview, because in many cases, that's exactly what it is!

It's The Soft Skills!

People almost never get fired from an internship because they don't know how to do something. You're not going to be canned because you didn't know how to run the copy machine or organize a computer database. When it comes to *hard skills* (the technical skills you need to know for a specific job), interns get a free ride. You're there to learn. If you already knew everything, you wouldn't be interning! It's the *soft skills* that can kill you.

Soft skills are those things you are just *supposed to know* – like you shouldn't talk with your mouth full or interrupt people when they are speaking. Unlike hard skills that you learn in school or on the job, soft skills are acquired through either life experience or through practice. We all begin learning soft skills when we are still children. They are the cues, both verbal and nonverbal, we pick up from our parents, teachers, and friends.

Soft skills include your ability to communicate, work as part of a team, act as a leader, solve problems, handle responsibility, and manage stress. There are many soft skills that your boss will expect you to have. Some you will possess. Some you might not. The scary thing about soft skills is that they can be totally subjective. What matters to one boss might not matter to another. Of course, no one is going to let you get away with freaking out and yelling in the workplace, but what about your team skills? Some employers will just want you to get the work done – period. They won't care if you work alone or as part of a group. Other managers will value your ability to work effectively with others.

Self Test: Your Soft Skills

Read through the following questions and rate yourself on a scale of 1 to 5, with "1" being weak and "5" being superior. After you complete the test, use the results to begin work on the soft skills that you need to improve.

If you really want to make this test effective, ask one or two people who know you to take the test, answering the questions about how they perceive you. See if their answers match how you view yourself. Remember, when it comes to soft skills, perception is reality.

_____ Do people consider me to be honest?

_____ Do people trust me with secrets? Do I have personal integrity?

_____ How well do I speak in groups or give presentations?

_____ How are my written communication skills? Can I express myself professionally, both in printed materials and in emails?

_____ Do I work well with others when trying to accomplish tasks?

_____ Can I work alone to meet deadlines? Do I have initiative or do I need to be reminded to get my work done on time?

_____ Do I try to solve problems instead of just figuring that some one else can fix them? Do I complete the work necessary to get the job complete or wait for another person to take over?

_____ Am I organized and methodical? Does being unorganized ever create problems in school, work, or my personal life?

_____ Am I good at problem solving? Do I look at all sides of an issue and hear what others have to say before making a decision?

_____ Can I handle stressful situations? Do I go with the flow or freak out when a problem occurs or plans change?

_____ Am I creative and open to new ideas?

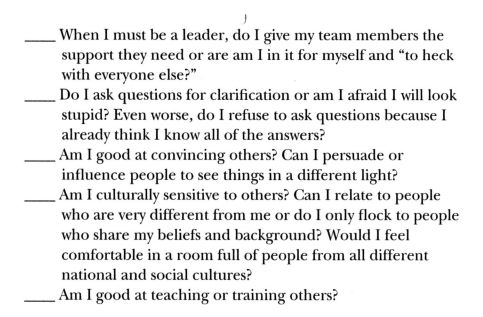

____ When I must be a leader, do I give my team members the support they need or are am I in it for myself and "to heck with everyone else?"

____ Do I ask questions for clarification or am I afraid I will look stupid? Even worse, do I refuse to ask questions because I already think I know all of the answers?

____ Am I good at convincing others? Can I persuade or influence people to see things in a different light?

____ Am I culturally sensitive to others? Can I relate to people who are very different from me or do I only flock to people who share my beliefs and background? Would I feel comfortable in a room full of people from all different national and social cultures?

____ Am I good at teaching or training others?

Hopefully, this self test will show you the soft skills that you should try to improve. It may also give you new insight to strengths you didn't even realize you had!

Why You NEED a Mentor

Everyone can work on improving some aspect of their soft skills. In fact, achieving better soft skills can be considered a life long process. For interns, the best way to bone up on your soft skills is to have a mentor. Hopefully, there will be someone at your internship who will act as your guide.

Don't have a mentor? Try to strike up a friendship with a person you admire and who is respected in the workplace. Don't be afraid to ask for their help. If you can't find someone at your internship, it is important to have a mentor in your chosen field or another professional who will listen to your stories about your internship and offer you advice and support.

Sample Dialogue:

Here is a sample dialogue on how to directly handle your request for a mentoring relationship.

(On her second day interning in the accounting office of a big hospital, Sara approaches a supervisor who seems especially welcoming and warm.)

"Hi," Sara says. "I'm really excited about this internship and I want to learn as much as possible. I also want to make you glad you gave me this opportunity. So, I'd like to ask you for some help."

"Sure," her supervisor replies. "Go for it."

"Well," Sara says. "You seem like the type of professional I would like to be someday and I respect your work. If you see that I'm doing something that isn't right, please let me know. I'm not just talking about the specific tasks I need to do, like checking invoices. I'm talking about the stuff that will help me become a real professional. For instance, don't be afraid to tell me if I'm talking too much or if I seem disorganized. I am not asking you to baby-sit me or hold my hand. I know you are way too busy for that. But I would like you to be honest about how I present myself."

"I would be happy to help you," the supervisor says. "In fact, I'm really impressed that you would even come to me in this way. As long as you don't mind honesty and can take constructive criticism, I have no problem pulling you aside from time to time to give you advice."

Building a true mentoring relationship takes time, but Sara is off to a good start. We'll talk more about the importance of mentors in the next chapter.

I Can't Believe You Wore That!

One of the biggest, most damaging mistakes interns make is wearing clothing that is too casual, flashy, or revealing. It doesn't matter what you like to wear. It only matters what is deemed acceptable in the workplace culture. What is fine to wear in one place might be totally wrong in another professional environment. However, a good rule to follow is *always dress for the job you want, not the job you have.* Ignore what your peers (the other interns) are wearing. Only pay attention to what the professionals in your office are wearing. It doesn't matter how much money you paid for those hot stilettos or Von Dutch sneakers – save them for your personal life. Don't wear them to your internship.

Before starting your internship, ask about the dress code. Your supervisor or human resources department should be able to help you. No matter what you are told, always avoid clothing that:

- Reveals too much cleavage, your back, your chest, your stomach or your underwear
- Looks wrinkled, torn, dirty, or frayed
- Has words, terms, or pictures that may be offensive to other employees or customers

What is "Casual"?

Knowing what to wear can be especially difficult during summer internships when many workplaces adopt more casual attire. Even in a workplace that has "casual Fridays" or a relaxed dress code, never make the mistake of being *too casual.* You must always project a professional, business-like image. If you can see yourself wearing a piece of clothing at the beach or to the gym, a club, or a sporting event, it is probably not appropriate for work.

It doesn't matter how good you are at your job if you are wearing a shirt that shows your belly or pants that hang around your butt. You will immediately be dismissed as a "kid," or even worse - tacky, sleazy, or a thug.

Slacks, Pants, and Suit Pants: In more casual workplaces, slacks that are similar to Dockers or nice dress pants are acceptable. Inappropriate slacks or pants include jeans (unless you are specifically told jeans are okay), sweatpants, exercise pants, shorts, bib overalls, leggings, and any spandex or other form-fitting pants such as bike clothing.

Skirts, Dresses, and Skirted Suits: Dresses and skirts that are split at or below the knee are acceptable. Dress and skirt length should be no shorter than a few inches above the knee, or a length at which you can sit comfortably in public. Short, tight skirts that ride halfway up the thigh are inappropriate for work. Mini-skirts, skorts, sun dresses, beach dresses, and spaghetti-strap dresses are ALWAYS inappropriate for the office.

Shirts, Tops, Blouses, and Jackets: Casual short sleeve button-down shirts with collars, polo shirts with collars, and dress shirts are acceptable. Most suit jackets or sport jackets are also acceptable attire for the office. Inappropriate attire includes tank tops; sweatshirts; midriff tops, shirts with potentially offensive words, terms, logos, pictures, cartoons, or slogans; halter-tops; tops with bare shoulders; and t-shirts unless worn under another blouse, shirt, or jacket.

Shoes and Footwear: Loafers, flats, oxfords, dress heels, dressy sandals and leather deck shoes are acceptable. In casual settings, wearing no stockings is generally acceptable if the look is appropriate to the outfit. However, more formal companies may require female employees to wear stockings year-round. Athletic shoes, thongs, flip-flops, and slippers are not acceptable in the office.

Jewelry: All jewelry should be in good taste, with no visible body piercing other than pierced ears.

Hats and Head Coverings: Hats are not appropriate in the office. Head Covers that are required for religious purposes or to honor cultural traditions are exceptable.

PARENT'S CORNER: YOUR CHILD THE PROFESSIONAL, NAVIGATING A NEW RELATIONSHIP

Now that your child is becoming a professional, you must be prepared to treat him or her as one. Yes, they will always be your baby in your heart, but when they walk out of your door, they are adults in the eyes of the rest of the world. Many times, even well-meaning parents will derail their children's internship opportunities.

Here are some important issues to consider when your child is looking for or obtains and internship:

• Let them go. Don't discourage them from taking internships in other cities or abroad. This is a big issue with parents. Often parents discourage their children from leaving home because they are more concerned with their own feelings and fears. They don't want to be separated from their kids or they are afraid their precious babies will not be able to cope so far away from home. Don't make this mistake. If your child feels like you are not being supportive, he or she might not take the internship and will miss out on a valuable opportunity.

For instance, if you daughter wants to work in fashion and you live in Iowa, she is probably going to have to move if she wants to be successful. Iowa may be great, but it is hardly the fashion capital of the world. Conversely, if you live in a big city on the East coast, don't discourage your son from taking a job in a small Midwestern community – even if you are afraid he will be the only African American in town or he will miss his favorite hangouts. Sure, the town's diversity and culture will be different from your city, but it may be the right move for him. In fact, he may even find out that he loves rural life and wants to stay. In the worst case, he will hate it and want to come home as soon as the internship is over. That's okay too. It will still be a valuable learning experience. Let your children make their own decisions and take their own risks.

- Encourage unpaid internships. Think long-term, not short-term. Unpaid experience can be very important and serve as a springboard to a paying job or internship.

    If you don't think your child can live without a paying job, help them come up with a plan. Perhaps they could work during the nights or weekends and limit their unpaid internship to a few weekdays. Maybe you think this sounds unrealistic because you are thinking, "My child needs to earn money!" You may be right, and of course money is important. Just don't force your child to write-off an opportunity because you think they should be making cash. When it comes time to find a job in their field, potential employers will want to see that they have real experience. Time spent flipping burgers will not look as good on a resume as relevant job skills gained at an unpaid internship.

- Respect your child as a professional. Don't ask your child to leave their internship to run errands for you or come home unless it is a true emergency. Often we hear horror stories about parents who called their children 20 times a day while they were working. Maybe you are used to calling their cell phones and being able to get a hold of them whenever you want to chat. This has to stop now!

    Don't put your kids in a bad situation because you want to come first in their lives. For example, one young lady we know did not go to an interview because she promised to have lunch with her mother! Her misplaced sense of responsibility cost her an important opportunity.

    Also, don't tell you kid that he needs to visit his Aunt Millie when he flies to Cleveland for a job interview because she lives in the area. That's not why he is going there! His first priority must be getting the job, not socializing with friends and family.

    Your children will never want to disappoint you, so they will often do things that will please you, even if those things are not in their best interest. Bottom-line: encourage them to be professionals and never ask them to do things that could be detrimental to their career.

6

INTERN TO "IN!"

Tamesha had a big decision to make. She had been offered an internship in Connecticut in the law department of an insurance company. Not only was it close to New York, where she wanted to be, it was a paid gig. She didn't think life could get any better until she got offered another internship – at the White House!

"I applied for the White House internship," Tamesha says. "But I never thought I would really get it. They offer those positions to very few people and it is very prestigious. Everyone just assumed I would be crazy not to decline the internship at the insurance company and head to Washington. What student would turn down an opportunity to spend the summer working inside the White House?"

Yet, that's exactly what she did. She told the White House "Thanks, but no thanks."

"I believe that all that glitters is not gold. My gut told me that I didn't want to go to the White house," she explains. "The internship in Washington D.C. was not paid and I would have to provide my own housing. It would be a financial strain on my family and my grandmother was sick at the time. Plus, the internship in Connecticut allowed me to take classes at a different university over the summer and allow me to see another type of college environment."

The decision to go to Connecticut literally changed the course of Tamesha's career. Until that point, she had wanted to become a lawyer. However, once she started working in a real law department, she was bored. Suddenly a life in the legal world didn't seem glamorous anymore. Tamesha could have chalked up the internship as a mistake, completed her hours, and moved on. Instead, she used the opportunity to find out what she did want to do for a living.

Tamesha says, "I realized that I was good at talking to people and training them. So, I went and volunteered in the human resources department. The people who worked in that office always seemed to be doing fun and interesting projects, like student book drives. I still worked in my own department – which I hated! But I talked to my boss and the director of human resources and asked if I could help the HR department during my downtime. *All I had to do was ask.* No one is going to turn down free help."

While volunteering in the human resources department, Tamesha concluded that she did not want to go to law school. That was a big, scary decision to make because all of her coursework had prepared to work in the legal field, not have a career in human resources.

Tamesha says that interning in the law department was the best thing she ever did because it showed her what she *didn't want to do.* Today, she is loving life as the Associate Director of Leadership Development for the Thurgood Marshal College Fund. Her job consists of training and providing career counseling for students. It fits her perfectly!

"The most important thing you need to know about an internship is that it will tell you if you are majoring in the wrong subject," Tamesha says. "The problem with college is that it doesn't allow for 'do-over's.' Once you pick a major, typically you are locked in unless you want to spend a lot more time and money to change it. In other words, if you go to college for four years planning to be a biologist, you can't just decide overnight to be an accountant. My internship taught me that I wanted to work with people, but my college training was preparing me for something completely different. Instead of changing my major and starting from scratch, I set my own career path. I relied on mentors and the research I received during my internships to get me where I am today."

Many students are thrilled when their internship confirms what they want to do for a living. For instance, Jake has always wanted to work on Wall Street. He is majoring in finance and has no "Plan B." Before his first day at his new internship with a large brokerage company, he became terrified.

"I kept thinking, 'What if I hate this? How can I know I want to work as a stock broker if I have never stepped foot in a brokerage firm?' It was scary to commit to a career that I didn't know much about," Jake remembers.

Fortunately, Jake's internship gave him a chance to prove to himself that he is very good at working under pressure and has a talent for understanding financial strategies. He discovered that his strengths and interests were perfectly matched for a job as a stock broker.

Self Test: Reassessing Your Future

Now that you have your internship, it's time to reassess your future. Has the reality of working there made you more certain that you have picked the right field or has it made you question your choice? Start by coming up with a list of strengths you have demonstrated at your internship. Examples of these strengths may include:

1. Strong organizational skills

2. Above average communication skills

3. Ability to meet deadlines

4. Good at scientific research

You get the idea. Try to come up with at least three or four things that you either didn't know about yourself or strengths that you confirmed by working at your internship. Write them in the space below.

    1. _____

    2. _____

    3. _____

    4. _____

Next, list your interests and dislikes. What do you enjoy the most about your internship? Is there something you discovered that you didn't like? Tamesha's list might have looked like this:

Interests:
1. Talking to people
2. Training employees
3. Coordinating corporate events
4. Acting as a liaison between the corporation and the public
5. Organizing charitable events, such as the book drive, blood drives, and employee donations to the United Way.

Dislikes:
1. Spending long hours preparing briefs
2. Working on individual projects instead of group projects
3. Lack of interaction with people outside of the department
4. Learning complicated corporate law regulations

In the space below, write the interests and dislikes that have become apparent during your time at your internship.

Interests:

    1. _____

    2. _____

    3. _____

4. _____
5. _____
6. _____

Dislikes:

1. _____
2. _____
3. _____
4. _____
5. _____
6. _____

Finally, look at both your strengths and your interests/dislikes and consider if they compliment your chosen field. During your internship, you should have gotten an idea of what skills various positions require. Let's say you want to be a computer programmer but you are not very good at math and you have gotten mediocre grades in the few basic programming courses you have taken. If your internship reinforces your belief that you need to have strong math skills to and be able to grasp certain programming concepts, it might be time to pursue an area more suited to what you can do well.

Don't stress out over this self-test. There are no right or wrong answers. The goal of the test is to get you seriously thinking about your future career. The more information you consider about yourself and your chosen field, the happier you'll be with your ultimate decision. Remember, it is easier to change career paths now than after ten years of working in an industry you don't like.

Networking

"It's not what you know, it's who you know." You've probably heard that before. Is it true? Yes and no. It is more accurate to say,

"It's who you know and who knows you." Throughout your career, never underestimate the importance of networking.

Many people have the misconception that networking is nothing more than collecting business cards and shaking hands. That's not networking! Networking is the proactive process of building relationships. It is the ability to act as your own public relations agent and develop a list of professionals who know your name and can vouch for your abilities.

Networking is one of the most important aspects of your internship. This is the perfect time to meet with people who are already working in the field you want to pursue. They can give you valuable insight into the corporate world and introduce you to other professionals. Networking also ensures that you will be remembered by key leaders in the company. It will be much easier to later ask for a job, request references, or keep in contact with the organization if you establish positive relationships during your internship.

There are many ways you can develop your network. One of the best places is at company events, such as receptions, luncheons, and informal office gatherings. People are usually already in the mood to talk and they will welcome a chance to chat with you. So, when you are involved in any kind of function, don't just sit around and talk to the other interns. Circulate!

If you know that there is a major office event coming up in your internship, develop a game plan before you go. Figure out a few people you want to meet. In most social situations, you are not going to be able to monopolize much of their time, so plan to be brief.

Sample Dialogue:

"Good Afternoon Mr. Jones. My name is Rebecca Marsha and I'm an intern in the finance department. I know that you've been with the company for a long time and have been very successful."

Then, after you exchange some pleasant small talk, say, "Thanks for talking with me. I know there are many other people here who want to speak with you. Perhaps I could sit down with you sometime and get some advice on how to begin my career. I would love to get some words of wisdom from you."

This conversation will demonstrate three things:
1. You are polite and professional
2. You value his time and are not overbearing
3. You are serious about your career

Not only will you gain real insight by this type of networking, you might also land a job. The next time there is an entry level opening, who is Mr. Jones going to hire? You or the other finance intern he never spoke to?

If there is not a major corporate function you can attend, strike up similar conversations in other places, like elevators, hallways, or during lunch. Just remember, if the individual looks like he or she is in a rush or is in the middle of a conversation with someone else, don't pounce. Wait until they appear relaxed and open to a discussion with you.

Not to do list - Networking

- **Don't assume people will help you just because they say they will.** This happens all of the time. You meet people who promise to look at your resume or make a few phone calls for you. Then nothing happens. Maybe they got too busy or just forgot about you. Even worse, maybe they just told you what you wanted to hear but never intended to follow-up on their promises. Don't rely on others to network for you.
- **Don't expect people to track you down.** It is your responsibility to keep networking relationships going. Very few people are going to spend hours trying to find you if they hear about an

opportunity you could benefit from. Make it easy on them by always providing your updated contact information.

- **Don't think you can get the same results by reading classified ads.** Many jobs and internships are never advertised. By creating a network of professionals, you'll hear about more opportunities. You want to get to the point where you don't have to fill out applications or send resumes because someone has already told a potential employer how great you are. If you don't have contacts, no one can do that for you.
- **Don't treat your contacts like casual friends.** The contacts you develop during networking are professional relationships, not personal ones. Don't use your networking conversations as an opportunity to complain about your boss or share overly personal information. You never know who people know or how your conversations could burn you in the future.

Finding a Mentor

A mentor is more than a contact. Your mentor is the person who acts as your advocate and can guide you and give you job-related advice.

Your mentor might:
- Help you with your resume
- Help you prepare for interviews
- Advise you on how to handle a difficult situation at work
- Be honest with you and offer constructive criticism. A mentor is the person who will not hesitate to pull you aside and say, "Why on Earth are you wearing that sloppy T-shirt to work?"
- Teach you new skills
- Assist you in developing a career path

Tamesha was lucky enough to find a mentor very early in her career.

"My mentor is the person who hired me and gave me my first job," Tamesha says. "She was my supervisor. At first she was just my boss – not my mentor. You never want your boss or supervisor to be your mentor. That's a conflict of interest. Plus, you never want to have a heart-to-heart conversation with your boss. That's not professional! When I left the company, I kept in touch with her and we developed a more personal relationship. She became my mentor. I trust her to give me advice about my professional development. The relationship has been very helpful and rewarding."

Notice that Tamesha did not consider her former boss a mentor until after she left the company. This is extremely valuable advice. Interns or entry-level professionals often make the mistake of being too comfortable with their bosses, especially if the boss is young and shares similar interests. You should always be professional and conservative in your relationship – no matter what your supervisor says or does. Even if your boss tries to engage you in more personal conversations, think carefully on how to respond. You need to strike the right balance. Remember, this is business.

Bottom-line: Having a mentor in the workplace or same profession is extremely valuable. Just make sure it is someone who does not directly supervise you. After all, what if you need help finding a new job or dealing with a difficult boss? You can't turn to your mentor for help if they are the one who is giving you trouble.

Finding a Champion

There is a difference between having a mentor and a personal champion. Your mentor is usually public knowledge. People in the office know who you talk to and eat lunch with. Your mentor is your friend. In contrast, a champion is the person who is your *private advocate.* Your champion is someone who wants you to succeed and is in the position to directly help you with your career advancement.

Imagine the company where you are interning has created a new, paid job opportunity that would be perfect for you. Your mentor might tell you about the position. However, when the people in charge of hiring have a meeting to decide who gets the job, it will be your champion who fights for you.

How do you get a champion? It's simple – do good work and impress the right people. You may not always know who all of your champions are. However, if you consistently demonstrate a strong work ethic and get results for the organization, people will take notice. Do a great job in your internship, mix in a little networking, and you'll develop champions.

Intern to "In"

Your internship can open the door to many other opportunities, both inside the company you have worked for and in other organizations. Before your leave your internship, think about how you can use it as a springboard to the next step in your career. As you approach your final days as an intern, make sure to:

- Meet with your supervisor, mentor, and champions individually   to get feedback on your performance. Ask what you did well and what areas you need to work on. Be open to honest criticism.
- Update your resume to reflect your new experience. Make sure to list your accomplishments and the skills you acquired. Many colleges require you to keep an internship journal. A journal is a great idea because it allows you to track your progress, which makes updating your resume easier.
- Figure out what you want to do next. Would you benefit from interning at the same company again? A multi-year internship with a company can increase your chances of getting a full-time job there once you graduate. If you do not want to return, use the experience to decide what other opportunities you want to explore.
- Ask for references. Don't hesitate to ask your supervisors, mentors, and champions if you can list them as a reference

on future applications. Ask for a letter of reference from a supervisor only in relation to a specific internship or job. Having a general letter of reference that does not apply with your future aspirations is useless.

Time to Get Paid!

You've done everything right and now you've landed an interview for a real job. Congratulations! One of the first things you are probably wondering about is the size of your first paycheck. Slow down! There are some important dos and don'ts in this situation.

Before you go on an interview or accept a job, start by researching what the average salary is for that position. Consider your level of experience and the region where you will work. Don't compare apples to oranges. For instance, jobs in New York City will pay more than jobs in Alabama because of the huge difference in the cost of living. You can find this information on a variety of websites. Just do a quick search or go to sites like Monster.com or CareerBuilder.com. Your university's career center is another source for reference material. Your mentor might also be able to give you some insight on the job market. Craigslist.org is another useful site to begin to learn about an area's housing prices.

Once you know what the going rate is, you need to think long and hard about what salary you will accept. What three amounts will make you walk away from the offer, accept the job, or make you scream like you just hit the jackpot?

Because salary is a sensitive subject, don't talk about it during the first interview. Most hiring managers will not discuss compensation until they are ready to offer you the position. However, it is a good idea to research the company and find out if they are posting the salary. If their ad says they pay $25,000, you don't want to say $40K if you are asked to state your salary requirements. Keep your salary expectations in line with what you already know about the specific position and the industry in general. Work out a budget beforehand so that you understand what you need to earn to survive.

If you are offered the job and the salary is not what you hoped for, ask for a day to think about it. As an entry-level candidate, you may be in a tough spot. It's not like you can negotiate a higher rate based on your years of experience or impressive track-record. I'm not saying you can't ask for more – just be realistic. You may get moving expenses or a bigger sign-on bonus, but you probably are not going to get a salary that is double the initial offer. Also realize that offers are not just about salary. They usually include a host of benefits, including paid vacation, health insurance, and retirement plans.

If you must decline an offer, be honest and do it formally. Even if you explain your decision verbally, follow-up with a letter so they can never say you didn't notify them. You never know when you might want to work with them in the future. If you learn only one thing from this book, it should be *never burn bridges*!

BUYING INTERNSHIPS

In June, 2006 Ellen Gamerman wrote an article for The Wall Street Journal profiling the disturbing trend of purchasing internships. Across the country, small and large corporations alike are auctioning off internships. The companies include names most us have heard of, such as In Style magazine and JP Morgan Chase financial services. Some of the internships are auctioned for thousands of dollars.

Gamerman wrote, "An internship this summer at In Style magazine 'is the perfect prize for someone interested in advertising sales, marketing or the magazine industry,' says the auction catalog for the Cosmetic Executive Women

Foundation's December fundraiser. At Cincinnati Country Day School, the auction described an internship at luxury-goods maker Louis Vuitton as 'a great opportunity to make contacts'."

The proceeds usually go to a charity and the lucky students who have parents willing to fork-over the cash get a great opportunity. It's a win-win situation, right? Wrong.

All interns suffer from this practice. College students who have worked hard and deserve an opportunity may be denied a chance simply because they didn't have the money to buy a position. Students who purchase the internship do not learn the value of hard work. They are also robbed of having an authentic internship experience.

If you are a parent, I'm sure you want your child to have their ability to stand on their own and succeed through their own merit. How does buying them an internship accomplish that goal? If you purchase the experience, they may get special treatment that they did not earn. Why teach your children to expect something they did not have to work for? They might also be respected less by people in the organization who say, "That kid doesn't deserve to be here. I don't look at him in the same way as those who were legitimately hired."

The auctioning of internships appears to be a recent phenomenon. For those who can afford it, it may seem like a reasonable way to get ahead. However, no matter how well-intentioned companies and parents are, the entire process sends a terrible message to all students, whether they come from rich, middle-class, or disadvantaged families. That message is: Don't worry about working hard during college. If your parents have the bankroll, you can buy impressive experience for your resume. If you can't afford it, you'll just have to work even harder for the fewer slots now available. That's life.

Do you really want to send that message?

CONCLUSION:
YOU'RE ON YOUR WAY

There isn't one sure-fire method to achieve the career of your dreams. However, there are no better, rock-solid investments in your future success than getting a college education and making the most of an internship. Study after study has proven that people with college degrees earn on average much higher salaries than those without degrees. That proves you need that piece of paper.

Yet, at Thurgood Marshall College Fund we know that a college degree is usually not enough. Lots of people flounder after graduation, with no real job prospects. That's because even with great grades and a degree from an impressive school, you need experience. Otherwise, you're likely to become another college graduate working as a clerk at the mall.

An internship puts you ahead of the competition. Today, young people are more in touch with technology than any other generation. While technological know-how is important, it can never replace the face-to-face networking and valuable communication, problem solving, and analytical skills you can learn as an intern.

By building these skills now, you'll be far less likely to ever hear a potential employer say, "Thanks for your interest, but we're looking for someone with more experience."

Your college degree will open many doors for you. Your college degree combined with internships will open the flood gates.

I wish you much success as you start a very exciting journey – your career awaits you.

RESOURCES

Internet Resources:

Thurgood Marshall College Fund
www.thurgoodmarshallfund.org

Inroads
www.inroads.org

Sponsors for Educational Opportunity (SEO)
www.seo-usa.org

United Negro College Fund (UNCF)
www.uncf.org

NAACP
www.naacp.org

National Black MBA Association
www.nbmbaa.org

Office of Personnel Management
www.opm.gov

Hadad, Roxana and Kay Peterson. Making the Most out of Your Internship. 28 May 2005
<http://fastweb.monster.com/fastweb/content/focus story/1542.ptm>.

Compiled by Steve Watson former Director of Internships at The King's College in New York, NY.

http://paidinterns.com/
Paid internship listing.

http://internships.wetfeet.com/home.asp
Internship Programs.com. Terrific site with many NYC media opportunities. Focused on internships.

http://idealist.org/
Idealist.org is a company where non-profit organizations send internships descriptions. Great site for government and non-profit jobs. Lots of international, too. Easy to search. The organizations range from Doctors Without Borders to the United Nations to Revive Baseball in Harlem (RBI) to the Public Broadcasting System. This link is an especially good resource that presents opportunities to serve the poor.

http://www.careerbuilder.com/
Career Builder. Lots of other job-related info.

http://www.vault.com/index.html
The Vault has excellent job listings for internships and other jobs. There is a gold level membership with monthly fees ranging from $3.95 to 5.95. There also are many interesting publications for sale.

http://ministrylist.com/
Careers in ministry.

http://www.manhattan-institute.org/html/internships.htm
The Manhattan Institute is a think tank whose mission is to develop and disseminate new ideas that foster greater economic choice and individual responsibility. Summer internship applications are due January 30th

http://www.heritage.org/About/Internships/index.cfm
The Heritage Foundation Internship Website

http://www.atr.org/aboutatr/associates.html
Americans for Tax Reform Internship Website

DWAYNE ASHLEY

CEO & PRESIDENT OF
THURGOOD MARSHALL COLLEGE FUND

A 19-year non profit veteran, Mr. Ashley has created and developed programs to benefit thousands of youth. Throughout his career, his fundraising advocacy for higher education and youth programs have generated more than $100 million.

In 2000, he created the Thurgood Marshall College Fund's Leadership Institute which has served more than 2000 students to date. The program is a model for preparing students to secure internships and jobs. Out of the program, he developed the HBCU Talent Sourcing Program designed to prepare students for "On Boarding" into a career.

Mr. Ashley is a sought after expert in the field of youth leadership and talent development.

Throughout his career, he has overseen the management of internship, scholarship and soft skills training programs that serve thousands of students. He has delivered more than 1,000 speeches on education, leadership and non profit management.

He currently serves on the Board of Directors of the Gallup Organization, a renowned leadership organization; Ronald K. Brown, Evidence Dance Company; Commissioner for the City of Newark's Historic Preservation Commission and serves as a member of the American Council on Education's Higher Education Secretariat.